Greetings! Crystals are a great way to help kids learn about energy, and the properties of the many different types of crystals out there.

In this book, we'll be exploring the top 10 crystals for beginners, aged 5 through 10, and why they are so important.

Getting children as young as five involved in learning about crystals can be an incredibly rewarding and beneficial experience for them.

Crystals have been used for thousands of years for their natural healing, spiritual and emotional properties, and teaching children about them at an early age can encourage them to develop an interest in these topics.

Here are some of the important benefits of introducing children to the world of crystals:

First, learning about crystals can help children to develop an appreciation for the natural world. Crystals are found in nature and learning about them can help to nurture children's connection with the environment.

Crystals are also powerful tools for teaching children about the power of intention and self-care.

Exploring the properties of different crystals can help children to understand the importance of setting intentions, taking care of their bodies, and creating a sense of balance and harmony in their lives.

Second, learning about crystals can also help children to develop their creativity and imagination. Crystals come in a variety of shapes, sizes, and colors and exploring these can help to spark children's curiosity and creativity.

They can be used to make jewelry, decorations, or just to explore the different aspects of a crystal. This can help to stimulate their imaginations and provide a fun way for them to express themselves.

Third, learning about crystals can help to teach children about the importance of self-care. Crystals have been used for centuries for their healing properties and understanding the power of these can help children to learn about the importance of self-care and healing. Crystals can also be used to help children understand the power of intention and how to manifest their desires.

Finally, learning about crystals can help to develop children's spiritual connection. Crystals have been used for centuries in spiritual practices, and exploring their properties can help to nurture children's spiritual growth. Learning about crystals can provide children with a greater understanding of the power of the natural world and how to use it to create a sense of connection and balance in their lives.

Overall, getting children as young as five involved in learning about crystals can be a rewarding and beneficial experience.

Crystals can help to nurture children's connection with the environment, stimulate their imaginations, and teach them about the power of intention and self-care, the power of intention and self-care. Exploring the properties of crystals can also help to develop children's spiritual connection and understanding of the natural world.

In short, crystals can be a great way to introduce kids to the wonderful world of self-care and mindfulness.

Now, let's get started with ten of the best crystals for young beginners!

Rose quartz is a beautiful pink stone that encourages love, kindness and compassion

Rose Quartz is known as the "love" stone, and is full of loving, calming energy. It is a great crystal to help learn about the power of love and self-acceptance.

Amethyst is a purple stone that is believed to increase focus and concentration, while helping to calm and relax.

It is known to be a great stone for stress relief, and can help kids stay balanced.
iIt is often associated with the third eye chakra, which helps us to open up to new experiences.

1. Rose Quartz is what color?
    a. Purple
    b. Blue
    c. Pink
2. What is Rose Quartz known as?
    a. Being pretty
    b. The Love Stone
    c. Rosey
3. Amethyst is what color?
    a. Orange
    b. Pink
    c. Purple
4. Amethyst is supposed to help you with stress.
    a. True
    b. False

Citrine is a crystal of abundance and prosperity. It can help kids to understand the power of manifestation, and the importance of setting intentions.

It is believed to bring success, joy, and optimism into your life. Citrine can be used to help with decision making and to manifest your dreams.

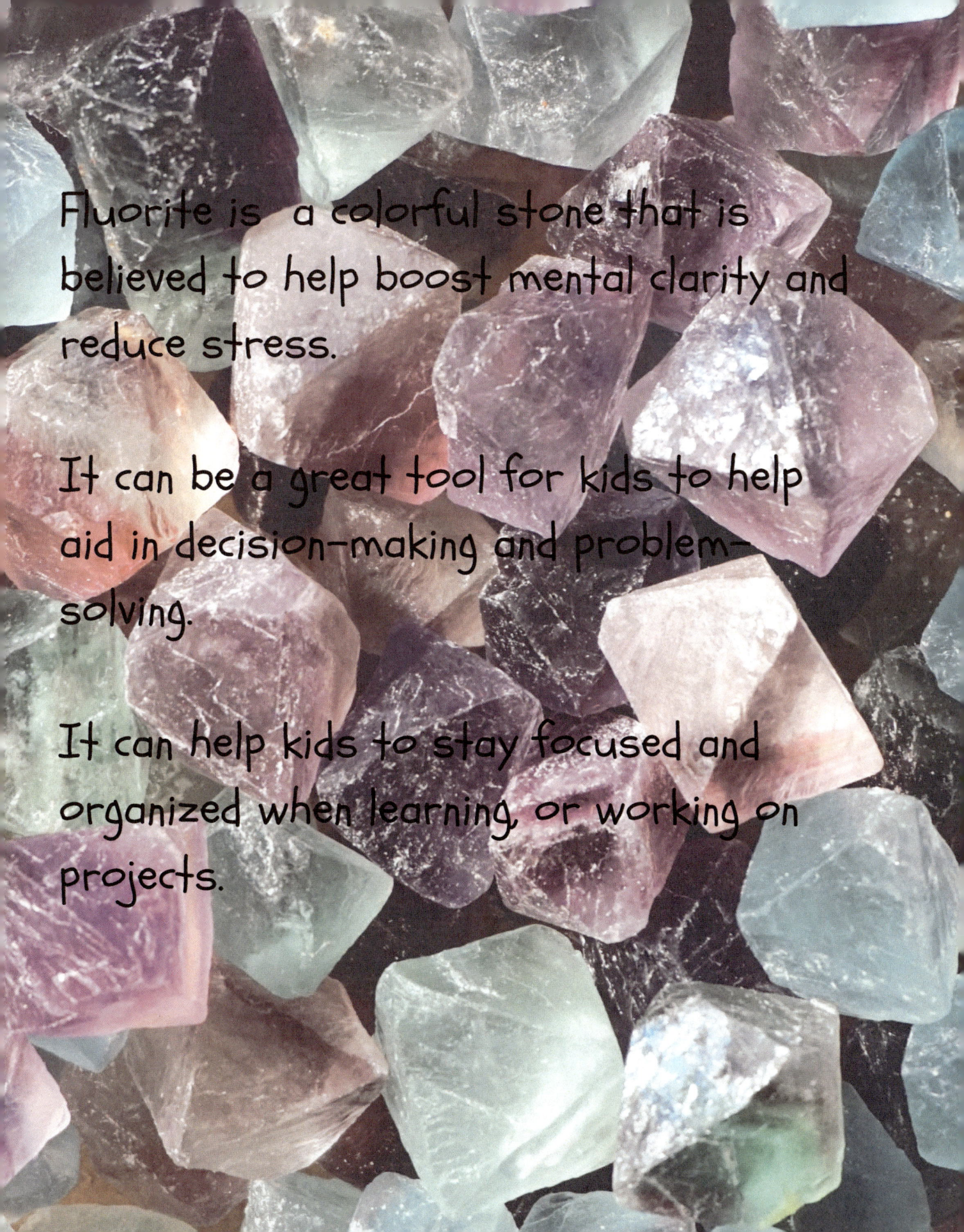

Fluorite is a colorful stone that is believed to help boost mental clarity and reduce stress.

It can be a great tool for kids to help aid in decision-making and problem-solving.

It can help kids to stay focused and organized when learning, or working on projects.

1. Fluorite is only one color.
    a. True
    b. False
2. Citrine and Fluorite helps with making decisions.
    a. True
    b. False
3. Citrine is orange in color.
    a. True
    b. False
4. Which is your favorite crystal so far?

    Rose Quartz   Amethyst
    Citrine   Aventurine

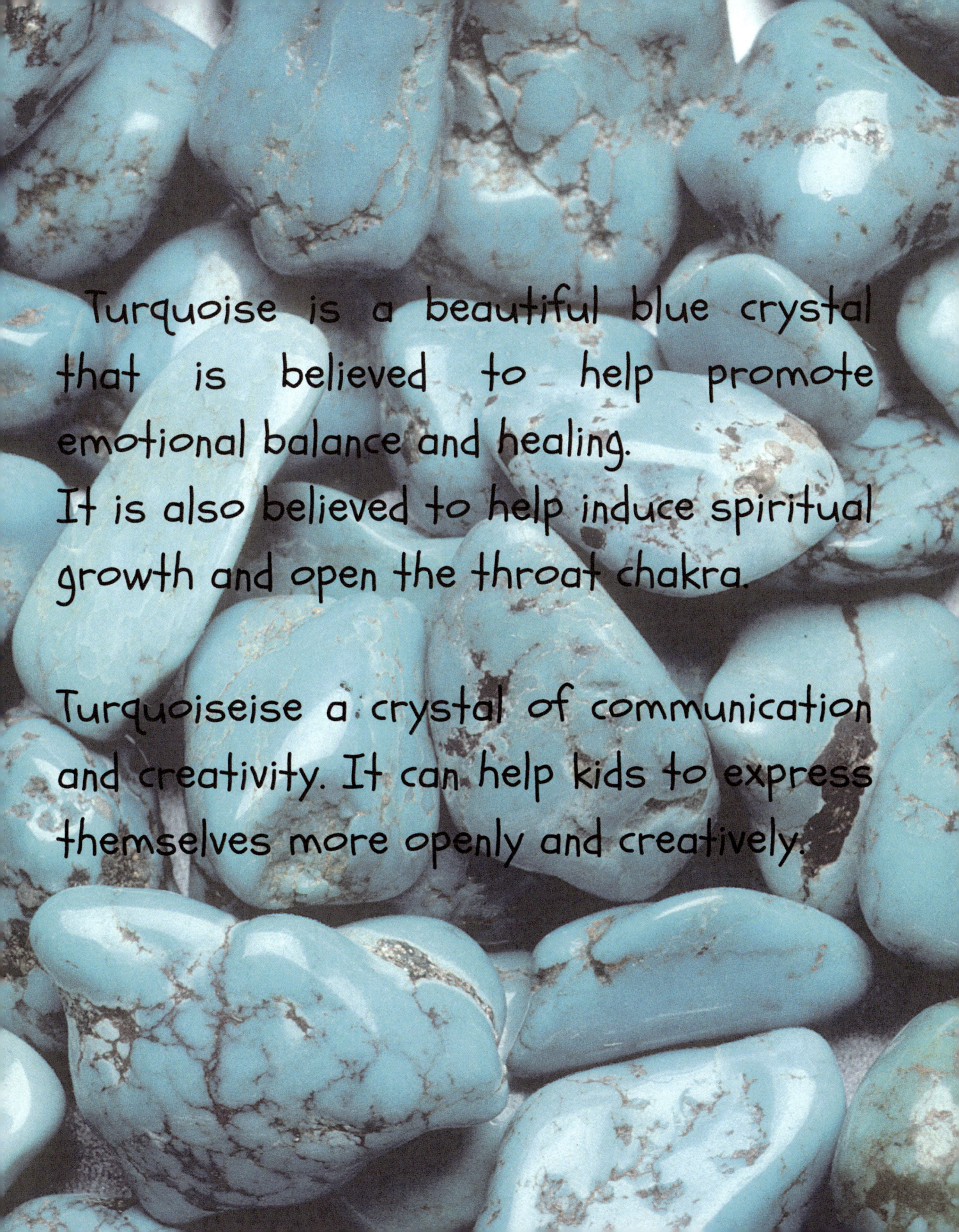

Turquoise is a beautiful blue crystal that is believed to help promote emotional balance and healing.
It is also believed to help induce spiritual growth and open the throat chakra.

Turquoiseise a crystal of communication and creativity. It can help kids to express themselves more openly and creatively.

Aventurine is a green crystal that is believed to help promote luck and prosperity.

It is also believed to help provide emotional balance and clarity.

It can help kids to understand the power of positive thinking and manifesting their desires.

What have I learned?

1. Turquoise is a beautiful yellow stone.
   a. True
   b. False
2. Aventurine helps with understanding positive thinking..
   a. True
   b. False
3. Turquoise is a crystal of communication and creativity.
   a. True
   b. False
4. Which is your favorite crystal so far?

Tiger's Eye is a golden stone that is believed to increase mental clarity and sharpen perception.

It can help kids stay grounded and focused, while inspiring them to take action.

It is believed to bring courage, strength, and stability. Tiger's eye is often used to help reduce fear, worry, and anxiety

Clear Quartz is a powerful stone that is believed to amplify energy and intention.

It is known to be a great stone for healing and can help kids stay connected to their spiritual side.

Clear Quartz is known as the "master healer" crystal. It can help kids to experience healing and balance on all levels.

What have I learned?

1. Tiger's Eye helps keep you grounded and focused.
    a. True
    b. False
2. Clear Quartz is known as the "Master Healer".
    a. True
    b. False
3. Tiger's Eye is known to help reduce anxiety.
    a. True
    b. False
4. Which is your favorite crystal so far?

Carnelian is an orange stone that is believed to bring courage and confidence. It is known to be a great stone for motivation and can help kids stay focused and determined.

It is believed to bring creativity, motivation, and optimism. Carnelian is often used to help you take action and to manifest your goals.

Sodalite is a blue stone that is believed to be a powerful aid for communication.

It is known to bring harmony and help kids be more assertive.

What have I learned?

1. Sodalite is blue in color and helps with confidence.
    a. True
    b. False
2. Carnelian orange in color and helps you stay focused.
    a. True
    b. False
3. Sodalite helps with being more assertive and Carnelian with taking action.
    a. True
    b. False

Did you know?

Crystals need to be charged and cleansed.

Selenite is a powerful crystal that can be used to cleanse and charge other crystals. It has a strong connection to the moon and is often used to bring harmony and balance. To cleanse and charge other crystals, simply place them on top of a piece of selenite or hold the selenite in your hand and move it over the other crystals. This will help to clear away any negative energy and fill the crystals with positive energy. Kids can also use selenite to help them focus and stay grounded during times of stress.

If you don't have selenite, you can still charge your crystals! All you need is the sun or moonlight. Place your crystal somewhere that it can get direct sunlight or moonlight, such as a windowsill. Leave it there for at least 3-4 hours. During this time, the crystal is absorbing the energy from the sun or moon and is recharging. When you're done, your crystal is ready to use!

Below are a five clues to a crystal I know you'll love. Let's see with some help from your mom or dad, if you can figure it out.

1. I'm a shiny gray rock that has magical rainbows inside of me!
2. I'm found in igneous and metamorphic rocks, so you might need to look hard to find me.
3. I'm often used to make jewelry, so I might be in the jewelry box!
4. I'm usually named after Labrador in Canada – it's where I'm most often found.
5. I'm a special kind of rock that can create a special kind of light..

Manufactured by Amazon.ca
Bolton, ON

34834081R00017